FUN FAX
Beginner's guide to
French

Compiled by Susannah Bradley

Illustrated by Rebecca Archer

Henderson Publishing

Woodbridge, England

BEGINNERS GUIDE TO FRENCH

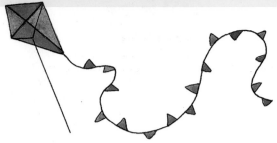

IF you are learning French at school you will find that these pages are a great help. They are not meant to be a French course in themselves but an aid to help you over the early stages of learning the language.

BEGINNERS GUIDE TO FRENCH

Masculine and Feminine

Remember that, in French, all nouns (words which name things) are either masculine or feminine. In front of each noun is '**le**' or '**la**'; these are the two French words for 'the'. '**Le**' is the masculine version and '**la**' is the feminine, so you can tell by this whether the noun after it is masculine or feminine. You cannot tell from the plural, because in both cases it is '**les**'; and if a word begins with a vowel, it becomes '**l**''.

Adjectives (describing words) change their form depending on whether they are used with a masculine or feminine noun. For example, **le melon sucré** (the sweet melon) but **la poire sucrée** (the sweet pear). Most feminine adjectives simply have an 'e' added to the masculine, but this is not always so; the word for beautiful is '**beau**' in the masculine and '**belle**' in the feminine, for instance. Adjectives usually come after a word, but not always. Some which come before the noun are:

BEGINNERS GUIDE TO FRENCH

autre	other
beau	beautiful
bon	good
gentil	nice
grand	big
jeune	young
joli	pretty
long	long
mauvais	bad
petit	small
vaste	enormous
vieux	old

When writing French, do not forget that accents are important. Those are the little marks above and below certain letters, as in le garçon, l'âge, and après.

BASIC WORDS

Some words are used often in sentences and to ask questions. If you learn them now, you can use them throughout these pages.

C'est . . .   it is . . .
Qu'est-ce c'est?
   What is that?
Qu'est-ce . . .?
   What is . . .?
aussi   also
Bonjour   Hello
Ça va?   How are you?
bien   well
très bien   very well
assez   enough
assez bien   quite well
pas très bien   not very well
très mal   awful

ils   they (masculine)
elles   they (feminine)
(use '**ils**' for a mixture of males and females)
il y a   there is, there are
oui   yes
non   no
jamais   never
peut-être   perhaps
quelquefois   sometimes

NUMBERS

un	one
deux	two
trois	three
quatre	four
cinq	five
six	six
sept	seven
huit	eight
neuf	nine
dix	ten
onze	eleven
douze	twelve
treize	thirteen
quatorze	fourteen
quinze	fifteen
seize	sixteen
dix-sept	seventeen
dix-huit	eighteen
dix-neuf	nineteen
vingt	twenty
trente	thirty
quarante	forty
cinquante	fifty
soixante	sixty
soixante-dix	seventy
quatre-vingts	eighty
quatre-vingt-dix	ninety
cent	a hundred
mille	a thousand
un million	a million

ALL ABOUT YOU

un garçon a boy

Je m'appelle Paul. Comment tu t'appelles?

As there was only room on the page for one person, we had to choose whether to draw a boy or a girl. If you're a girl — sorry!

la tête head
les cheveux hair
la peau skin
l'oeil eye
le nez nose
la bouche mouth
les dents (f) teeth
la poitrine chest
le bras arm
le doigt · finger
le pouce thumb

la main hand
la jambe leg
le genou knee
le doigt de pied toe
le pied foot
la cheville ankle

> **What he is saying:**
> My name is Paul.
> What's your name?

ALL ABOUT YOU

les cheveux frisés
    curly hair
une frange   a fringe
il porte des lunettes
    he wears spectacles
les cheveux blonds
    fair hair
le chien   dog

drôle   funny
remuer la queue   to
    wag its tail
le chat   the cat
l'homme   man
ronronner   to purr
sympathique   friendly
la moustache   moustache

What they are saying:
Paul: How old are you, Sophie?
Sophie: I am eight years old.
Marc: My name is Marc. I am the same age as Sophie.

8 FRENCH

THE FAMILY

la famille the family
le père father
la mère mother
le frère brother
le grand-père
grandfather
la grand-mère
grandmother
l'oncle uncle
le cousin boy cousin
la cousine girl
cousin
la soeur sister

What they are saying:
Sophie: Here is my family.
Grandmother: She is my granddaughter.
Aunt: She is my niece. The baby is my nephew.

NOTE: How to say 'my':
If the word has le in front, change it to mon.
If it has la in front, change it to ma.
If it has the plural, les, change it to mes.

FAMILY EVENTS

la naissance   birth
naître   to be born
Maman   Mum
Papa   Dad
la fête   party
le gâteau   cake
le ballon   balloon

les noces   wedding
la mariée   bride
le marié   bridegroom

le cadeau   gift
les noces d'or
   golden wedding

What they are saying:
Baby: Waaaah! — it's the same in any language!
Wedding guest: Congratulations!
Grandma at birthday party: Happy birthday!
Grandpa at Golden Wedding: Thank you very much.
Guests at birthday party: Hello.

THINGS PEOPLE DO

le marin sailor
le soldat soldier
le mannequin
model

le médecin doctor
la marchande
shopkeeper
le curé clergyman
l'ouvrier (m) labourer

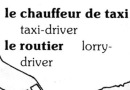

l'avocat lawyer
l'agent de police
policeman
le boueux dustman

le chauffeur de taxi
taxi-driver
le routier lorry-
driver

THINGS PEOPLE DO

le pompier   fireman
le coiffeur   hairdresser
le fermier   farmer

le chef de cuisine
   the cook
le directeur de
   banque   bank
manager

le caissièr / la
   caissière   cashier
le facteur   postman

l'acteur   actor
l'actrice   actress
le chef d'orchestre
   musical conductor

THE HOUSE

le toit roof
la maison house
l'immeuble (m)
  block of flats
l'appartement (m)
  flat
le balcon balcony
la porte d'entrée
  front door

la cheminée
  chimney
sonner à la porte to
  ring the bell
la sonnette doorbell
la voisine neighbour
la fenêtre window

J'habite cette maison. Où habitez-vous?

J'habite un appartement.

Moi aussi.

What they are saying:
Paul: I live in this house. Where do you live?
Sophie: I live in a flat.
Marc: Me too.

NOTE: How to say 'this':
Say ce instead of le, cette instead of la and ces instead of les. For a masculine word beginning with a vowel, use cet.

THE KITCHEN

la cuisine kitchen
la machine à laver
  washing machine
faire la vaisselle to
  wash up
repasser to iron
sale dirty
l'évier (m) sink
faire la lessive do
  the washing

le placard cupboard
le verre glass
le pain bread
le thé tea
la tasse cup
la fourchette fork
le couteau knife
la cuillère spoon

What they are saying:
Paul: These plates are clean now, Mum.
Mother: Good, Paul.

THE LIVING-ROOM

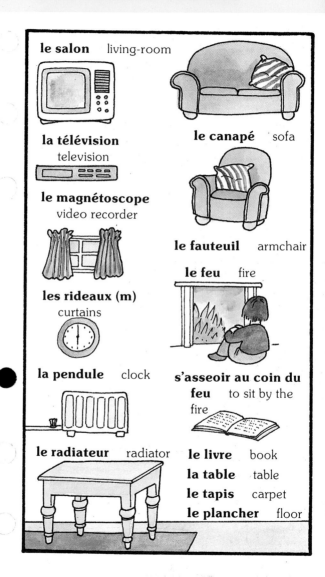

le salon   living-room

la télévision
television

le magnétoscope
video recorder

les rideaux (m)
curtains

la pendule   clock

le radiateur   radiator

le canapé   sofa

le fauteuil   armchair

le feu   fire

s'asseoir au coin du feu   to sit by the fire

le livre   book
la table   table
le tapis   carpet
le plancher   floor

THE BEDROOM

Bonne nuit, Paul.

Mais, Papa, je voudrais un verre de l'eau, s'il vous plâit.

la chambre à coucher bedroom
le lit bed
le reveil alarm clock

le peignoir dressing-gown
le pullover jumper
la chemise shirt
le pantalon trousers
aller se coucher go to sleep
le pyjama pyjamas
les pantoufles (f) slippers
la couette duvet
dormir to sleep
rêver to dream

What they are saying:
Father: Good night, Paul.
Paul: But, Papa, I want a glass of water, please.

THE BATHROOM

la salle de bains
bathroom
prendre un bain to
have a bath
éclabousser to
splash
la balance scales
le bouchon plug
le savon soap
la brosse à dents
tooth-brush
se brosser les dents
to clean your teeth

le robinet tap
l'eau (f) water
chaud/e hot
froid/e cold
le dentifrice
tooth-paste
le rasoir razor
la glace mirror
la serviette towel
la douche shower

THE GARDEN

le jardin   the garden
faire le jardinage   to do the gardening
la pelouse   lawn
le parterre   flowerbed
le jardin potager vegetable garden
la tondeuse lawnmower
la fleur   flower

la mauvaise herbe weed
l'arbre (m)   tree
l'oiseau (m)   bird
la serre   greenhouse
le buisson   bush

Où est le cerf-volant, Paul?

C'est perdu.

Quel dommage!

What they are saying:
Marc: Where is the kite, Paul?
Paul: It's lost.
Sophie: What a shame!

GOING SHOPPING

le grand magasin
department store

l'escalier roulant (m)
escalator

le prix   the price

le reçu   receipt

la cliente   female
customer

la vendeuse   female
shop assistant

cher   dear

le jouet   toy

les vêtements (m)
clothes

acheter   to buy

What they are saying:
Customer: I would like to buy . . .
Assistant: Certainly, sir.

SHOPPING FOR FOOD

la boucherie
butcher

l'épicerie (f)
grocer

la boulangerie
bakery

la poissonnerie
fishmonger

l'étalage (m) market
stall

faire la queue to
queue

la charcuterie
delicatessen

la pâtisserie cake
shop

le supermarché
supermarket

J'ai une liste et j'ai un sac à provisions.

What she is saying:
I have a list and I
have a shopping
bag.

UNPACKING THE SHOPPING

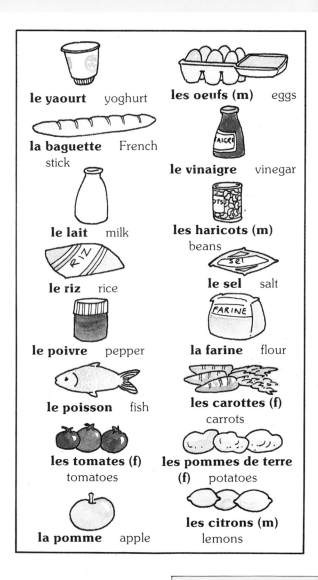

le yaourt   yoghurt

la baguette   French stick

le lait   milk

le riz   rice

le poivre   pepper

le poisson   fish

les tomates (f)   tomatoes

la pomme   apple

les oeufs (m)   eggs

le vinaigre   vinegar

les haricots (m)   beans

le sel   salt

la farine   flour

les carottes (f)   carrots

les pommes de terre (f)   potatoes

les citrons (m)   lemons

AT THE POST OFFICE

la poste post office
la lettre letter
envoyer to send
la boîte aux lettres
  post box
par avion air mail
la fiche form
le timbre stamp

le colis parcel
le porte-monnaie
  purse
le sac à main
  handbag
l'argent (m) money

MAKING A PHONE CALL

téléphoner to make a telephone call

le téléphone telephone

numérotez dial the number

le numéro de téléphone telephone number

l'annuaire (m) telephone directory

au revoir goodbye

raccrocher to hang up

en cas d'urgence in case of emergency

appeler police secours call for the police

où êtes-vous? where are you?

Allô . . . qui est à l'appareil?

What Sophie's Mum is saying:
Hello . . . who is speaking?

ASKING THE WAY

Pour aller à . . . ?
Which way is . . . ?
droite right
gauche left
tout droit straight on
tournez . . . turn . . .
prendre to take
c'est loin? is it far?
à côté de next to
la rue the street

la première rue the first street
la deuxième rue the second street
la troisième rue the third street
l'église (f) the church
là-bas over there
Pardon Excuse me
Merci Thank you
Je vous en prie You're welcome

Est-ce que l'église est loin d'ici?

Lentement, s'il vous plaît!

Allez tout droit jusqu'à la boucherie, puis prenez la deuxième rue à gauche, puis —

What they are saying:
Man: Is the church far from here?
Paul: Go straight on at the butcher's, then take the second street on the left, then . . .
Woman: Slowly, please!

AT SCHOOL

l'école (f) maternelle
nursery school
l'école primaire
primary school
le lycée secondary
school
l'université (f)
university

la salle de classe
classroom
le directeur
headmaster
le cours course
l'élève pupil
au lycée at school
lire to read
écrire to write
la cour de récréation
playground
le cahier exercise
book
la trousse pencil–
case
la règle ruler
le crayon pencil

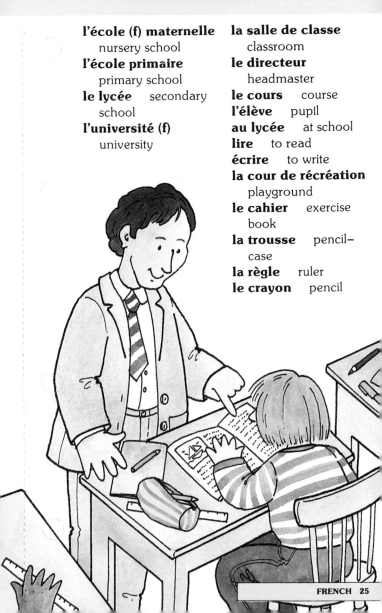

AT SCHOOL

le trimestre term
la rentrée beginning of term
la fin de trimestre end of term
l'emploi du temps (m) timetable
l'orthographe (f) spelling
le mot word
la phrase sentence

l'informatique (f) computer studies
l'histoire history
la géographie geography
la chimie chemistry
la physique physics
la musique music
la gymnastique gymnastics

l'ordinateur (m) computer
le clavier keyboard

OUT IN THE CAR

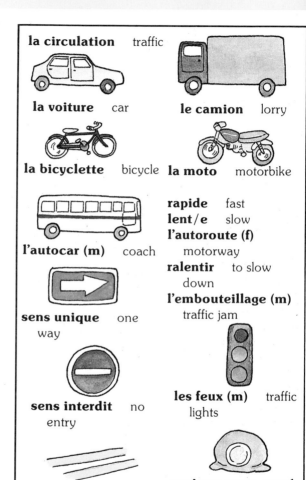

la circulation traffic

la voiture car

le camion lorry

la bicyclette bicycle

la moto motorbike

rapide fast
lent/e slow
l'autoroute (f) motorway
ralentir to slow down
l'embouteillage (m) traffic jam

l'autocar (m) coach

sens unique one way

sens interdit no entry

les feux (m) traffic lights

Stationnement interdit! No parking!

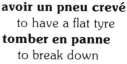

avoir un pneu crevé to have a flat tyre
tomber en panne to break down

GOING BY TRAIN

le train train
la gare station
le guichet ticket office
le billet ticket
réserver une place to reserve a seat
le chef de train guard

à l'heure on time
le wagon-lit sleeping-car
le rapide inter-city train
le filet luggage-rack
Non-fumeurs Non-smokers
le quai platform
la voie track
l'horaire (f) timetable

AT THE AIRPORT

l'aéroport (m)
airport
l'avion (m)
aeroplane
voler to fly

les bagages (m) à main hand luggage

l'hôtesse de l'air
air hostess

le magasin hors-taxe
duty-free shop

l'étiquette (f) label

la valise suitcase
Rien à déclarer
Nothing to declare
la douane customs
le douanier
customs official
embarquer to board
le pilote pilot

le chariot trolley

le passeport
passport

TAKING THE FERRY

le port port
le carferry ferry
la traversée crossing
le mal de mer
  seasickness
charger to load
décharger to unload
la cale the hold
l'ancre (f) anchor

le hublot porthole
aller en bateau
  travel by boat
le pont deck
la cheminée funnel
la passerelle
  gangway
le capitaine captain

AT A CAFÉ

le garçon waiter
la carte menu
l'addition (f) bill
le pourboire tip
le plateau tray

un cola a coke
un verre de lait glass of milk
une glace ice-cream

un chocolat hot chocolate
un thé au lait tea with milk
un thé au citron tea with lemon
le fromage cheese
la viande meat
les pommes frites chips
la pizza pizza
la salade salad

Que desirez-vous?

Un jus d'orange et deux limonades, s'il vous plaît.

What they are saying:
Waiter: What would you like?
Paul: An orange juice and two lemonades, please.

FEELING POORLY

les fleurs (f)   flowers
vomir   to be sick
être enrhumé(e)   to
  have a cold
éternuer   to sneeze
avoir de la fièvre   to
  have a high
  temperature
l'ordonnance (f)
  prescription
le comprimé   pill
se sentir mieux   to
  feel better

Salut, Marc. As-toi mal au ventre?

Non, j'ai mal à la tête.

What they are saying:
Sophie: Hello, Marc. Have you got stomach-ache?
Marc: No, I have a headache.

THE TIME OF DAY

le matin   morning
l'après-midi   afternoon
le soir   evening
la nuit   night
midi   noon
minuit   midnight

Quelle heure est-il?
It is one o'clock
What time is it?
Il est une heure
It is one o'clock
Il est cinq heures
It is five o'clock

**sept heures moins le
    quart**   quarter to
    seven
**sept heures moins
    dix**   ten to seven
sept heures cinq
    five past seven
sept heures et quart
    quarter past seven
sept heures et demie
    half past seven

**Il est huit heures du
    soir**   It is eight
    o'clock in the
    evening

THE WEATHER

l'hiver   winter

le printemps   spring

l'été   summer

l'automne   autumn

il pleut   it's raining
la pluie   rain
il fait froid   it's cold
le tonnerre   thunder
la foudre   lightning
l'arc-en-ciel (m)
   rainbow
la grêle   hail
le gel   frost

la neige   snow
j'ai chaud   I'm hot
il fait du brouillard
   it's foggy
le vent   wind
il fait du vent   it's
   windy
le soleil brille   the
   sun is shining

Quel temps fait-il?

Il fait beau.

What they are saying:
Sophie: What's the weather like?
Mother: It's fine.

THE DAY AND THE DATE

Quelle est la date de ton anniversaire?

janvier January
février February
mars March
avril April
mai May
juin June
juillet July
août August
septembre
   September
octobre October
novembre
   November
décembre
   December

Mon anniversaire est le vingt-et-un avril.

dimanche (m)
   Sunday
lundi (m) Monday
mardi (m) Tuesday
mercredi (m)
   Wednesday
jeudi (m) Thursday
vendredi (m) Friday
samedi (m)
   Saturday

What they are saying:
Marc: What is the date of your birthday?
Sophie: My birthday is the twenty-first of April.

THE DAY AND THE DATE

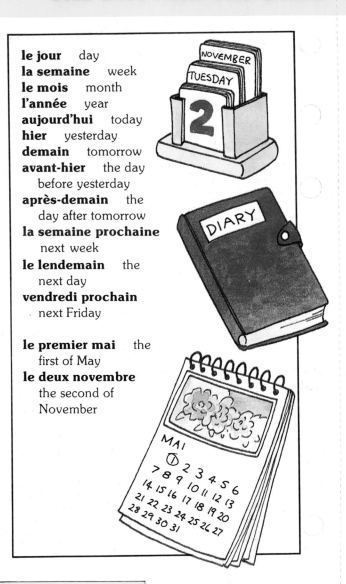

le jour day
la semaine week
le mois month
l'année year
aujourd'hui today
hier yesterday
demain tomorrow
avant-hier the day
  before yesterday
après-demain the
  day after tomorrow
la semaine prochaine
  next week
le lendemain the
  next day
vendredi prochain
  next Friday

le premier mai the
  first of May
le deux novembre
  the second of
  November

AROUND THE WORLD

le monde the world
le nord north
le sud south
l'ouest (m) west
l'est (m) east
le pôle nord North Pole
le pôle sud South Pole
le pays country
le continent continent
la Grande-Bretagne Great Britain
la France France
la Suisse Switzerland
l'Allemagne Germany
les Pays-Bas (m) Netherlands
l'Italie (f) Italy
l'Espagne (f) Spain
les États-Unis (m) USA
l'URSS (f) USSR
l'Inde (f) India
la Chine China
la Nouvelle-Zélande New Zealand
l'Australie (f) Australia
l'Amerique (f) du Sud South America

AT THE BEACH

au bord de la mer
at the seaside
le château de sable
sand castle
le seau bucket
la pelle spade
le rocher rock
le crabe crab
le coquillage shell
la mouette seagull
la vague wave

se baigner to swim
la plage beach
barboter to paddle
faire de la planche à voile to windsurf
les lunettes (f) de soleil sun-glasses

Deux francs.

Combien coûte une glace?

What they are saying:
Paul: How much is an ice-cream?
Ice-cream man: Two francs.

AT THE ZOO

le zoo   zoo
l'animal (m) sauvage
   wild animal
le zèbre   zebra
la girafe   giraffe

le bébé phoque
   baby seal
le pingouin
   penguin

le lion   lion
le tigre   tiger

le chameau   camel
l'autruche (f)
   ostrich

l'ours (m) blanc
   polar bear

l'éléphant (m)
   elephant
la défense   tusk
le singe   monkey

ON THE FARM

la barrière gate
le blé wheat
faire la moisson to harvest
le mouton sheep
le chien de berger sheepdog
l'agneau lamb

le champ field
le fermier farmer
le cochon pig
la grange barn
la vache cow
traire les vaches to milk the cows

Pas maintenant, Paul — dans une semaine.

Est-ce que tu fais la moisson, Grand-père?

What they are saying:
Paul: Is it harvest-time, Grandad?
Grandad: Not yet, Paul — in a week's time.

COLOURS

As these words are adjectives, they may be masculine or feminine, depending on which noun they accompany. That is why there is a choice of endings in certain cases.

la coleur colour
vif/vive bright
terne dull
pâle pale
foncé/e dark
rouge red
bleu/e blue
vert/e green
violet/te purple
orange orange
rose pink
noir/e black
blanc/blanche white
gris/e grey
jaune yellow

MEASUREMENTS

la hauteur height
mesurer to measure
le mètre metre
la largeur width
la longueur length

le volume volume
un litre a litre
un demi-litre half a
   litre

le poids weight
une livre half a kilo

la forme shape

la cercle circle

le triangle triangle

le carré square

HOBBIES

Je tricote I knit

J'aime faire la cuisine I like to cook

Je joue du piano
I play the piano

J'aime le sport
I like sport

Je fais de la peinture
I paint

Je danse I dance

Je regarde la télévision
I watch television

Je lis des livres
I read books

The verb '**jouer**' (to play) is tricky because you use it in two ways. Use '**jouer a**' when talking about playing a sport, but '**jouer de**' about playing an instrument. Remember that '**a**' plus '**le**' becomes '**au**' and '**de**' plus '**le**' becomes '**du**'.

EATING WITH FRIENDS

Sers-toi Help yourself

Voulez-vous encore . . . ? Would you like more . . . ?

J'ai assez mangé, merci I've eaten enough, thank you

C'est délicieux It's delicious

Tu peux me passer . . . Would you please pass me . . .

bien s'amuser enjoy yourself, have fun

À table! It's on the table!

avoir bien mangé to have eaten well

> *Merci. J'ai faim!*

> *Bon appétit!*

What they are saying:
Mother: Enjoy your meal.
Sophie: Thank you, I'm really hungry.

PRONOUNS

The

The clue to whether a French word is masculine or feminine lies in the word for 'the'. **'Le'** is used before masculine nouns and **'la'** before feminine ones. **'L''** is used before those beginning with a vowel. **'Les'** is used for plurals.

A or An

'A' or 'an' is **'un'** with masculine nouns and **'une'** before feminine ones.

My and your

To say **'my'** in French, put **'mon'** before masculine words and **'ma'** before feminine ones. The plural is **'mes'**. For **'your'** it's **'ton'** (masculine), **'ta'** (feminine) and **'tes'** (plural).

PRONOUNS

It
In French there isn't one word for 'it' —
again it depends on whether the 'it' is
masculine or feminine. '**Il**' is masculine,
'**elle**' is feminine. '**Ils**' and '**elles**' are the
plural versions.

Some
The word to use for 'some' is '**du**' before '**le**'
words, but it's '**de la**' before '**la**' words and
'**de l'**' before '**l'**' words. Use '**des**' in front of
plurals.

à plus le
When '**a**' comes before '**le**', say '**au**'.

PRONUNCIATION

This is a guide towards making the right sound.
It is better, though, to copy the accent of a
French person, if you can find one to teach you.

a	Like the 'a' in 'cat'
e	Like the 'a' in 'above'
é	Like the 'ay' in 'tray'
ê	Like the 'a' in 'care'
i	Like the 'ee' sound in 'peep'
o	Like the 'o' in 'cot'
u	Put your lips into an 'oo' position, but think 'ee' as you say it
eau, au	Like the 'oa' in 'coast
eu	Like the 'er' in 'her'
ou	Like the 'oo' in 'boot'
oi	Like the 'wa' in 'whack'
on, an	Like the 'ong' sound you have to make for the doctor as he examines your tonsils
un	Like the 'u' in 'bun' (the n is silent, though)

PRONUNCIATION

in, ain, im	Like the 'an' in 'rang' (the n is silent)
c	Before 'i' or 'e' it is like the 'c' in 'certain'. At other times it is as in 'cat'
ç	Like the 'c' in 'certain'
ch	Like the 'sh' in 'sheep'
g,j	Like the 's' sound in 'Asia'
gn	Like the first 'n' sound in 'onion'
th	Like the 't' in 'tap'
Qu	Like the 'k' in 'kite'
h	Always silent